Railways
on and around
DARTMOOR
Chips Barber

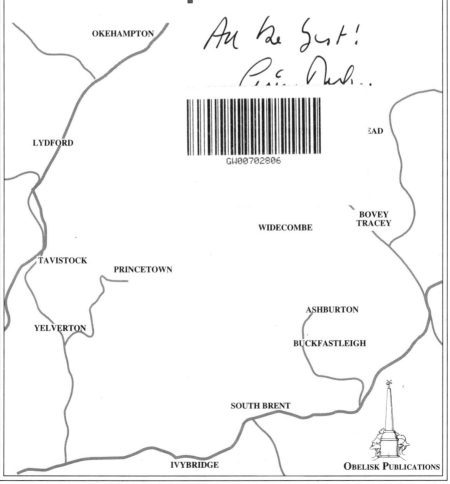

OKEHAMPTON

All the best!

Peter Park...

GW00702806

LYDFORD

ḶAD

BOVEY
TRACEY

WIDECOMBE

TAVISTOCK

PRINCETOWN

ASHBURTON

YELVERTON

BUCKFASTLEIGH

SOUTH BRENT

IVYBRIDGE

OBELISK PUBLICATIONS

Other titles by the Author include:

Diary of a Dartmoor Walker
Diary of a Devonshire Walker
The Great Little Dartmoor Book
Dark and Dastardly Dartmoor
Ten Family Walks on Dartmoor
Weird and Wonderful Dartmoor
Beautiful Dartmoor
Six Short Pub Walks on Dartmoor
Widecombe – A Visitor's Guide
Around and About the Haldon Hills – Revisited
The Great Little Exeter Book
Made in Devon
The Ghosts of Exeter
The Great Little Totnes Book
Tales of the Teign
The Great Little Plymouth Book
Plymouth in Colour
Ghastly and Ghostly Devon
Dawlish and Dawlish Warren
Torquay / Paignton / Brixham
Ten Family Walks in East Devon
Around and About Salcombe
Burgh Island and Bigbury Bay
Beautiful Exeter
Dartmouth and Kingswear
Cranmere Pool – The First Dartmoor Letterbox
The Great Little Chagford Book
Haunted Pubs in Devon

We have over 150 Devon-based titles – for a list of current books please write to us at
2 Church Hill, Pinhoe, Exeter, EX4 9ER telephone (01392) 468556

ACKNOWLEDGEMENTS

Special thanks to Anthony R. Kingdom, Colin Burges, Ron Lumber and
the *Western Morning News*.

PLATE ACKNOWLEDGEMENTS

With thanks to the following for either lending, originating or taking the pictures in this book:
Lens of Sutton, Chapman and Son of Dawlish, Jane Reynolds (for drawings), Chips Barber,
Mavis Piller, Rosie Oxenham, Tom Bolt, Mike Wreford, Paul Ash, Mrs Pritlove, Sue and Richard
Callow, Jill Fitzsimmons and P. Zabek. Title page map created from out-of-copyright source.

Front cover picture is The South Devon Railway at Buckfastleigh. Back cover picture is of
the sculpture *Waiting for the Train* by John Butler, found at Bideford Station.
Photos by Chips Barber.

First published in 1997 by
Obelisk Publications, 2 Church Hill, Pinhoe, Exeter, Devon
Designed by Chips and Sally Barber
Typeset by Sally Barber
Printed in Great Britain by
The Devonshire Press Ltd, Torquay, Devon

Railways on and around Dartmoor

Railways and their routes have always been of interest to me. Although I was just a child when most branch lines lapsed into closure, I was fortunate that my grandfather 'worked on the railways', because rail travel was either cheap or free for members of our family. Consequently my grandmother used to take me on many railway journeys into 'the back of beyond' on various lines in Devon. Of the ones featured in this book, I can vividly remember travelling from Exeter as far as Lydford, and also along the Teign Valley line many times. I can just about recall chugging (well, it was really the train that did the chugging) from Totnes all the way to Ashburton. Fortunately in the summer most of that journey can still be experienced on the South Devon Railway, but those last few miles into Ashburton are now buried beneath the A38, 'the Devon Expressway'.

This book is not meant to be a definitive guide to Dartmoor's passenger railways but just a brief and light-hearted encounter with them. Anyone who dreams of locomotives when asleep and daydreams about them when they are awake will already have a library full of railway books. They are the true railway enthusiasts who can quote trains, rolling stock, timetables of yesteryear, know to the nearest yard the length of long-gone platforms and the arrangement of station layouts, and who pursue their hobby with an impressive passion. But all that is attempted here is a brief look at the 'Railways on and around Dartmoor' to see their characteristics and peculiarities, to understand how the topography of the moor affected them and to conclude what their roles were in that ever-turning wheel we call social history. Several contemporary extracts from newspaper articles, about their genesis or exodus, have been included to show how they were welcomed or how enthusiasts said their 'goodbyes' to them.

Dartmoor is the highest area of South West England, a natural barrier to railroads, whose engineers must have baulked at the thought of the gradients and obstacles involved in getting around or over it. The clever and skilled use of cuttings, embankments, bridges and viaducts, in a terrain of hard resistant rock and high hills, deeply dissected by streams and rivers, meant that these lines created plenty of hard work for the armies of navvies engaged in building them.

ALONG THE SOUTHERN EDGE OF DARTMOOR

The first priority in Devon, in mid-Victorian times, was to link centres of population and as Dartmoor, populated by ponies, sheep and cattle rather than people, was a hilly hindrance, getting around it was more of a consideration than serving it. The first major rail route from Exeter to Plymouth only skirted the edge of the Moor, but from 5 April 1848 there were moorland-edge stations at Brent and Ivybridge. There was also a station at Wrangaton which bore the name of 'Kingsbridge Road' because it was the closest station to that lovely South Hams town. However, in December 1893 Kingsbridge's own branch line, from Brent, was opened and 'Kingsbridge Road' became 'Wrangaton'. Later others were added at Rattery, Bittaford Platform (shown here but closed 2 March 1959) and Cornwood (1852) on the southern edge of Dartmoor.

Ivybridge today is a fast-growing dormitory town, with its own 'Park and Ride' station, opened in 1994 to help reduce the daily flow of road traffic into Plymouth. The station is functional rather than ornate, with an immense car park, but it is not on the same site as the original station, which was farther west, one that Annan Dickson described in 1950.

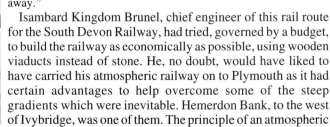

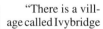

"There is a village called Ivybridge … where I never saw the siding used for anything but horseboxes; for that is where the Dartmoor always held their first Meet, after which they crowded up a steep stony lane to the Moor Gate – and away."

Isambard Kingdom Brunel, chief engineer of this rail route for the South Devon Railway, had tried, governed by a budget, to build the railway as economically as possible, using wooden viaducts instead of stone. He, no doubt, would have liked to have carried his atmospheric railway on to Plymouth as it had certain advantages to help overcome some of the steep gradients which were inevitable. Hemerdon Bank, to the west of Ivybridge, was one of them. The principle of an atmospheric

Railways on and around Dartmoor

railway was sound enough – it was just putting it into practice that was the difficult thing to do. The atmospheric experiences, of regular breakdowns, gained on the track from Exeter through Dawlish and Teignmouth to Newton Abbot, meant that the system was abandoned at great financial loss to the railway company. The decision to change to more conventional locomotives, ironically, came at a time when the 'teething problems' were just being sorted out. Even with 'ordinary' locomotives there would be problems and, sure enough, poor old 'Hercules', an evening goods train, didn't make it to the 'top' . Whilst toiling up the 1:42 gradient of Hemerdon Bank, a climb of 273 feet from the eastern outskirts of Plympton, in 1849, the driver, having put on more steam, only succeeded in pushing his engine beyond its capabilities and it 'blew up'.

Here are extracts from the newspaper report which followed the events of this railway's first day in the spring of 1848.

"The official opening of the line was fixed for Friday. By common consent all business in Plymouth was suspended, banks, shops, and all other places of trade, with but very few exceptions, being closed. The weather was most auspicious, and with the morning, which was ushered in by the merry peals of the church bells, came evident signs that the event was to be celebrated as a general holiday.

For the accommodation of the Directors and others officially connected with the works, and their friends, a private train started from the station at Laira [Plymouth] at ten minutes to eight (London time). This train consisted of one first class, two second, and two third class carriages, and completed the distance to Totnes in forty-two minutes. Here a substantial breakfast was prepared at the Seven Stars, and Seymour Arms Hotel, and the party having been joined by the Directors of the Great Western, Bristol and Exeter, and a number of other gentlemen who came down specially for the purpose, the opening train was started at 10.16 a.m. It was of great length, and drawn by two engines, the Pisces and Cancer, the former conducted by Mr Gooch... and the latter by Mr Rae..."

The entourage included a vast number of well-known gentry, almost a 'Who's Who' of mid-Victorian society from this part of the world.

"At 10.16 a.m. the train, gaily decorated with flags, started from Totnes, the inhabitants of which place, and others on the line, assembled in large numbers to greet it on its course. We have before stated, that nothing can exceed the beauty of the scenery through which the line wends its way – smiling meadows and richly wooded valleys alternate with woodlands and heath intersected with streams, here as placid as a vestal's dream, and anon noisy and turbulent, as it comes dashing onward from its mountain birth. No county can present a greater variety – there is perpetual change – the eye never tires. Leaving Totnes, the line passes through Follaton Park, the seat of Stanley Carey, Esq., and thence through Rattery to Marley, the residence of Lady Carew. Here there is a tunnel of 800 yards ... which was passed in less than a minute, but fleeting as time is, such is the aversion of human mind to darkness, that but for the indisputable evidence of the fact, the traveller might be dubious of the statement. Passing this we cross the first or Glase Viaduct, on to South Brent and Wrangerton [sic] to Ivybridge, where a viaduct 110 feet in height, is thrown across the valley of the river Erme. The scene in passing over this is beyond all description, and we were surprised indeed after all the awful prognostications issued in reference to these noble works, to find so heavy a train passing over without any visible change from the more solid way. The same must be said of the Slade viaduct of equal height, indeed the whole of the works throughout are of the most substantial and satisfactory character. As Plymouth is approached, additional interest is given to the scenery by this frequent succession of gentlemen's seats; amongst which are Beechwood, the residence of Colonel Mudge; Fursdon, the residence of T. Fox, Esq.; Goodamoor, the seat of Paul Treby, Esq.; Hemerdon, Capt. Woolcombe; Slade Hall, Capt. Pode; Elford Leigh, the residence of William Fox, Esq.; and lastly the beautiful domain of the Earl of Morley. At Plympton St Mary is a bridge which has excited the wonder of the local craft; as a piece of masonry it is probably unequalled in the kingdom, certainly not excelled, and the false prophets have pronounced the impossibility of its standing, but we are happy to say that here as with the line in general, the croakers have been most miserably disappointed. But a few years since it was said, our lovely county of Devon offered insurmountable difficulties to railway travelling – it was a penalty we were doomed to – her hills and valleys appeared to say to human integrity, 'so far and no further can you approach'. The skill and enterprise, however, of Mr Brunel have surmounted all of these difficulties – the irregularities the surface presented appear to have but increased this gentleman's determination to surmount them. With Napoleon he would hear of no such word as impossible; and we could not help thinking, as the train flew over hill and dale on Friday, of the proud feelings of that gentleman at success over such apparently insurmountable difficulties, and which was so loudly pronounced by the tens of thousands of persons assembled to greet the arrival of the opening train over the noble work now completed ...

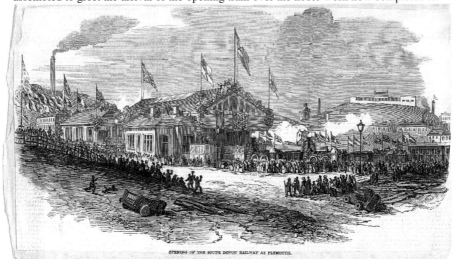

OPENING OF THE SOUTH DEVON RAILWAY AT PLYMOUTH.

At three o' clock a luncheon was provided at the Royal Hotel, Plymouth of which about eighty gentlemen partook ... The health of Mr Brunel was duly honoured..."

A close look at the current Ordnance Survey map shows that this railway, whose wooden viaducts were later replaced by masonry bridges built beside them, now forms the boundary line of the Dartmoor National Park from the bridge over the former A38 (now the B3213) just east of Bittaford, to Fardel Bridge, to the northwest of Ivybridge, before swinging away from the moor towards Plymouth. In the opposite direction it leaves the National Park by the impressive 869-yard-long Marley Tunnel on the Totnes side of this moorland-edge section.

This is where four men lost their lives in September 1846 when the line was under construction. On that fateful day John Poshills, Henry Bigwood, William Parnell and John Letcher had been working on the arch at the entrance to the tunnel. They were removing a supporting timberwork frame around it, everyone thinking that the tunnel entrance was secure, when there was a mighty crash as part of the arch collapsed, instantly killing the men. The tunnel was built because Lord Carew did not want the railway running through his estate so it was put underground to appease him.

On a happier note, South Brent Station, a short way to the west, was used for filming scenes from the film *I Live in Grosvenor Square*, a film released in 1945 with the American title *A Yank in London*. *Halliwell's Film Guide* described it as a "sloppily-made topical romance which was hot box office at the time…" It was about a Duke's daughter who fell head-over-heels in love with an American air force sergeant. It starred Anna Neagle, Rex Harrison, Robert Morley, Dean Jagger and the Exeter-born Irene Vanbrugh. The extras were paid a £1 a day at South Brent but double this if they were used in moorland scenes. More about this and many other films and television programmes shot in the county can be read in another of my books, *Made in Devon*.

The train ride from Exeter to Plymouth is a superb one and for those who like variety in the landscape it includes river, estuary, coast and moorland scenery, even if the route passes a little too close to the Moor to see much of it.

FROM NEWTON ABBOT TO MORETONHAMPSTEAD

The Dartmoor National Park encompasses an area of about 365 square miles and not all of it is open moorland. The former rail route from Newton Abbot to a once-remote Moretonhampstead would have provided glimpses of moorland, but also it would have passed through marshes, meadows, heaths, clay works, woods and fields on its way between the two places. Nevertheless, it would have provided the means for those travellers intent on healthy exercise, to easily reach the moors by alighting at Bovey Tracey or beyond.

The 12¼-mile-long branch line, built by the Moretonhampstead & South Devon Railway, was opened on 4 July 1866 and included here are excerpts from the *Exeter Flying Post*'s report from the following day. It not only tells us about the branch line, but also the times and attitudes in which it was established. It provides a detailed description of the topography through which the line passed. One rarely sees such wonderfully imaginative and descriptive reports like these any more. I suppose this sort of detail, in an age without radio or television, would have been welcome and avidly devoured.

"'Where is Moretonhampstead?' asks the tourist – planning a summer's ramble through the delightful scenery of Devon and selecting for a visit the pretty little country town on the borders of Dartmoor which seems to have grown up, no one but archaeologists know how, in the most out of the way nook of the county. The popular answer to this enquiry in Devonshire has long been that 'Moretonhampstead is twelve miles from everywhere,' which is true to this extent at least, that Moretonhampstead is twelve miles from Exeter, twelve miles from Newton Abbot, twelve miles from Okehampton, and twelve miles from Crediton. It is in the heart of a quadrilateral of market towns lying in a circle, most delightfully situate, barring the inconvenience of roads, in the midst of some of the prettiest scenery in Devon, and with a high reputation for the salubrity of its air. Physicians send patients there from all

parts of the country, tourists flock there like pigeons, yet with all its attractions Moretonhampstead, until yesterday, has been practically out of the world. Yesterday it was brought into the circle of railway civilisation. The South Devon Railway Company, with characteristic enterprise, have taken Moretonhampstead under their protection, connected it by a line of rails with Newton Abbot...

... The inauguration of the line took place yesterday morning; a train starting at eleven o' clock from Newton ...

There were the usual manifestations of rejoicings all along the line, immense crowds of people collecting at every conceivable and inconceivable point to see the train and cheer the passengers. If the engine had been the first seen in this part of the country it could not have excited more curiosity and excitement among the people. The day was delightful; the arrangements perfect; and the trip most enjoyable.

On the arrival of the train at the station hearty cheers were given by the numerous company assembled on the platform ... the address was read by ... the local secretary, congratulating the directors on their safe arrival by that steam horse and iron road now so essential and necessary for the progress and advancement of every neighbourhood...

The directors and committee headed by the Newton band then marched into the town, a distance of about half a mile. At Moretonhampstead the popular excitement and enthusiasm was brought to a culminating point in a variety of agreeable forms for the commemoration of the latest 'triumph of the steam engine.' The town was thronged with visitors. The streets had been broken up and the plantations thinned to furnish an avenue of firs for the decoration of the streets. The church bells rang merrily all day long and the ladies with thoughtful consideration, spread a long line of tea tables under the shadow of the firs for the entertainment of the poor and the villagers attracted to the town by the festivities of the day. The inhabitants also provided a luncheon for the entertainment of the directors and their friends, which was held in the Unitarian schoolroom, the hosts of the White Hart and White Horse being the caterers..."

There then followed a lengthy list of all the élite who enjoyed the lavish repast with a number of toasts, loyal and otherwise, and plenty of mutual self-back-slapping. As the paper stated: "Altogether the day passed off most successfully and pleasant."

But the article wasn't done yet, because it went on to tell its readers ...

"Sufficient funds were subscribed by the summer of 1863 to warrant the line being proceeded with. The country surrounding and along the upper portion of the line is remarkably fertile, and large quantities of agricultural produce will be brought over the line to the markets of Newton and Torquay – those markets being the most easy of access. It is supposed that the district is rich in minerals, including copper, tin and iron and the shipment of ores can be effected with facility at Torquay, Teignmouth and Dartmouth, and from those ports the Moreton district can be supplied with coal... The extensive pottery works at Bovey and the smelting works in course of construction in that locality in connection with the Bovey coal field may be expected to contribute largely to the traffic of the line.

The line passes through the properties of the Earl of Devon, the Duke of Somerset, Major Adair, John Divett, James Buller, W. R. Hole, W. Harris, J. Harris, Rev. N. Gould (Plumley), Rev. Mr Woollcombe, George Wills (Kelly), James Wills (Rudge), Thomas Wills (East Wrey), George Wills (Narracombe), Thomas Amery (Higher Coombe), T. White (Moreton), W. R. Crump (Wray Barton), J. Stevenson and J. S. Nosworthy. The works of art consist of ten overway and twenty five underway bridges and viaducts, besides numerous culverts and fourteen level crossings including those for private occupation...

There are two stations on the line ... at Bovey Tracey and Lustleigh. Probably there is no twelve miles of railway passing through any locality in the West of England possessing such fine and varied scenery as is to be witnessed between Newton and Moreton. The new line branches off from the South Devon line a short distance from the Newton station, crossing by two bridges the rivers Lemon and White Lake within a few yards of each other. The line is single throughout, although the overway bridges have been constructed and land has been inclosed for a second line... should it be required. At Bovey the line passes under a double-arched oblique bridge, while in a short distance at the left of it is situated the Bovey Potteries where several hundred hands are continually employed by Messrs Divett, Buller and Co. Bovey contains about 2,000 inhabitants, but the town is not very visible from the station on account of the number of trees of different descriptions it is surrounded by...

After leaving Bovey station the line passes through a shillet cutting at Staddon's-hill to the middle of another deep cutting of similar material in Park Wood. From this part of the railway Park House, the residence of W. R. Hole, Esq., surrounded by a magnificent park and commanding some very pretty scenery, attracts the passenger's notice. The line afterwards proceeds on a level for a short distance through Mr Harris's wood, when it again rises at the rate of one in sixty seven through a shillet cutting over an embankment at Woolford-bridge, through another cutting along the steep side of the hill to a spot where Yeo farmhouse previously stood. This farmhouse, lately occupied by Mr Fewing, was taken down in consequence of it's being found impracticable to divert the line either to the right or to the left of it...

Passing through Yeo Farm the line proceeds over embankments varying from ten to forty feet in height, and an oblique bridge at an angle of thirty degrees unto Letford-bridge. Scenery of a very romantic and imposing description here opens up; but it falls far short of what awaits the visitor as he proceeds further up the line. The moorland in continuation of Haytor Down extends to within a very short distance of the line of the railway. Near at hand is the celebrated Becky Fall, which was once a beautiful cascade, but whose waters are now greatly diverted to drive the machinery of some coal works at Bovey. The scenery at the Fall is very romantic, and at times when a surplus of water abounds the stream dashes in a fine foamy volume over a succession of granite rock boulders about seventy feet in height. The rivers Wrey and Bovey unite near this part of the railway. The next place reached is Knowle. After this the line passes through a small granite cutting, and then emerges over a two-arched viaduct and an embankment upwards of forty feet in height near Lustleigh Mill. A glimpse of an old mill and the valley beyond from under the viaduct has a very pleasing effect, while the little river rushing perpetually onward from the moor, now brown in shadow, now glittering in the sun, seems to sing a song of greeting to the traveller as it continues its course. Going through another deep cutting we cross over the Wrey to Lustleigh station on a level, leaving the parish church to the left. This is about eight and three quarter miles from Newton.

Within about half-a-mile from the station is Lustleigh Cleave, a place frequented by tourists. It is a wildness strewn with granite masses in strange confusion and unnumbered shapes among which is a logan stone called the "nutcracker," which can be made to logg with very little pressure. Lustleigh Cleave is at an elevation of about 1,000 feet above the line of the railway. It is also remarkable for its accumulation of granite boulders, extending nearly a mile over one of the highest hills in the neighbourhood. The line continues on a level till passing Bishopstone-bridge, when for about a mile and three quarters through Sandduck-wood it rises with the quickest gradient between Newton and Moreton, viz., one in forty nine. On leaving this bridge the line goes through a very rough country, the hills towering on either side of it to an immense height, covered here and there with woods of a varied description, and the barren parts are more or less covered in wild disorder with huge pieces of granite, some rising as high as twelve or twenty feet above the surface, the whole uniting in presenting one of the finest scenes for which this country is so justly noted. In the midst of this delightful neighbourhood resides Thomas Wills, Esq., one of the directors, and who, as one of the leading agriculturists of the neighbourhood, has done much towards raising the money for cutting the line. On leaving the slight cutting through Sandduck-wood the railway proceeds for some distance along the original bed of the river Wrey and some feet below it. Not only has the course of the river been consequently diverted, but it has also been considerably lowered below the railway in order to prevent the line being inundated during the winter months. From this spot the line rises to Moreton at an inclination of one in eighty-seven, one in eighty-two, and one in seventy-five respectively, until arriving within half-a-mile of the station, whence it continues on a level to the end."

And those who travelled the line could do so safe in the knowledge that the various structures along the line had been thoroughly tested. The Government Inspector of Railways, Colonel Yolland, with the help of two of the heaviest trains of the day, with carriages as well, gave three tests to each bridge. He ensured that each was sped over, crept over and stopped on, the line passing the test with flying colours.

The railway soon started to effect change. It helped to see off some of the toll roads in this district, it enabled moorland-edge folk to get to work in Newton Abbot, it opened up the latter's markets to a wider number of farmers and it served to make Eastern Dartmoor less of a remote area. However it also sped the departure of smaller markets and stirred others, who had been sedentary, to consider the advantages of more mobility. It made people living on the Dartmoor borderlands more aware of the time itself which, until the arrival of the railways, was a much more casual concept. It made employers of 'cheap labour' ponder the thought that 'loyal' servants might be prepared to travel for higher wages. Indeed, the arrival of a railway such as this, however modest in its scale, had an impact on the geography of this area. And it's probable that if the 'country cousins' had been more adventurous and the railway company better run, then the social revolution in and around the foothills of Dartmoor would have been more dramatic than it was. Newton Abbot, with its arrival, became even more of a junction town and grew accordingly, taking on a decidedly industrial appearance. The lower, non-Dartmoor section saw the most use, with a range of industries making good use of the line.

At Bovey, where 'better scenery' was encountered going northwards, it was possible for travellers to forsake the railway to climb aboard horse-drawn conveyances, like the one shown here, and visit places like Haytor and Widecombe. However, at times of excessive rainfall, gondolas would have been more appropriate because the nearby River Bovey regularly burst its banks and the line between the platforms was frequently flooded.

This branch line gradually grew in importance from its humble beginnings. In 1906 the Great Western Railway, who had taken over the running of the line in July 1872, introduced a connecting bus service to the thriving moorland town of Chagford. Day trips from London to Dartmoor became popular for those with the means and the inclination. Market day at Newton was a Wednesday and the trains were crammed with passengers, all with business to do in the busy South Devon town.

The long newspaper article, quoted earlier, mentioned the line passing the Parke estate

at Bovey Tracey, now the headquarters for the Dartmoor National Park. In the period between the death of Major Hole and the reoccupation of this house a television film crew came here to make a silent comedy film. *The Picnic* starred the Two Ronnies, Corbett and Barker, and was shown in 1975.

The line between Newton Abbot and Bovey crossed the generally flat and uninteresting Bovey Basin, close to the flood plain of the River Teign, through Teigngrace to reach Heathfield. This is where a junction was established with the Teign Valley line, featured later in this book. The remains of the station at Heathfield are immediately on the north side of the A38 Exeter–Plymouth highway but most of the passing motorists zoom by without knowing of the station's existence. Between Heathfield and close to Bovey a short platform, complete with wooden shelter and a few benches, known as Brimley Halt, was opened on 21 May 1928.

Another 'Halt', Hawkmoor, exactly 7 miles and 61 chains from Newton Abbot, was opened on Monday 1 June 1931. Its name was the same as the former tuberculosis hospital, a sanatorium where sufferers were brought. There was some dismay on behalf of passengers arriving here, to visit patients; they had expected a short stroll to the hospital, only to find themselves on something of a route march. The distance between halt and hospital, as the crow flew, was just about half a mile but the lanes took the wayfarer on quite a considerable detour. Until 1950 patients were met by a horse-drawn vehicle which conveyed them to Hawkmoor. A motor-van replaced it to add comfort and speed for those who were to be confined here. Not long before the railway was to close, the name of this stop was changed to 'Pullabrook Halt'.

Cecil Torr wrote a series of books under the title *Small Talk at Wreyland*, this being in Lustleigh, and his third volume, published in 1923, had this to say of the station.

> "Time seemed to be of very little value when I first knew the place. After the railway had been made (1866) my grandfather took his time from the station clock – he could see the hands with his big telescope, looking over from a stile near here. Till then he took it from a sundial.
>
> After the railway came, the trains proclaimed the hours, as most people knew the timetables approximately, calling the 8.19 the 8, the 11.37 the 12, etc. – odd minutes did not count. As the trains upon this branch were 'mixed,' partly passenger and partly goods, there was some shunting to be done; but this caused no delay, as the generous timetable allowed for it. If there was no shunting, the train just waited at the station until the specified time was up. The driver of the evening train would often give displays of hooting with the engine whistle while he was stopping here, and would stay on over time if the owls were answering back.

The engines on this branch were quite unequal to their work, and there were no effective brakes then. Coming down the incline here, trains often passed the station; and passengers had to walk from where the train stopped."

A year after the line opened Cecil's grandfather wrote this to Cecil's father, about a train bound for Moreton which was unable to cope with its load.

"On Saturday we had a runaway on the rails. The train passed here at 4 o'clock with two carriages, two trucks and a van, and could not get on further than Sandick road, so unhooked the trucks, and was not careful to secure them, and they went off and passed the station [at a] full 40 miles an hour. I was at the stile when they passed. Luckily they did no harm and stopped at Teigngrace, and the engine came back and fetched them."

There is a story that shows the gradient of the line being put to good use. Imagine the frustration of those who lived at Bovey Tracey wanting to have a night out, at a dance, party or ball in the Moreton area to discover that the last train 'home' was several hours too soon for them to have a good time. But there were those who worked out that the line

had quite a drop down through the Wrey and Bovey valleys and if a wagon, with a manual brake, could be arranged to be hauled on the last train up to Moreton then their transport home problem was solved. And thus it was that in the wee small hours of the morning that the revellers would rendezvous back at Moreton's station and climb aboard. The wagon would be pushed off into the darkness by some strong-armed locals, and after a sluggish, level start would gradually gather momentum as it sped through the night. With the skill of seasoned adventurers, they

apparently knew exactly when and where to apply the manual brake so that they would stop at Bovey. Here they would push the empty wagon into a siding, full moons making the journey a thrilling one. I wonder who worked the points for them? Whether this journey was done just the once or many times is not known, the daredevil party-goers remaining anonymous… Let's hope no locals took a late night short cut along the line!

However, legitimate walkers, in the parish of Lustleigh, were often induced to miss the train, and once more Cecil Torr was the narrator of a situation that could have been avoided.

"There is a new guidepost at Lustleigh. Instead of getting a larch pole that might have cost about five shillings [25 pence], the District Council got an iron post that cost five pounds; and on that post the sockets for the arms are at right-angles to each other. One arm is marked 'Cleave', and points along the road there. The other is marked 'Station', but (being at right-angles to the first) it points along the path to Wreyland, which path does not go anywhere near the station. Hence, many objurgations from excursionists when they have missed the train."

The station at Lustleigh once had, like many others, a station cat. When it had used up its full quota of nine lives it was buried in a little grave on the station platform. Its little gravestone, no longer in existence, carried this cute epitaph. "Beneath this slab and stretched out flat, Lies Jumbo, once our station cat."

Railways on and around Dartmoor

And there were also the 'Hounds', of the literary type, who came here in 1934. Some scenes for a version of *The Hound of the Baskervilles* were shot at Lustleigh station, but these were not for the famous Basil Rathbone version of 1939. Should you be fortunate enough to see it, then Lustleigh Station, 8 miles and 66 chains from Newton, is where the diminutive Lestrade, a detective, alights from the train on his way to team up with Sherlock Holmes and Watson.

If you had fancied a holiday with a difference, then the railway siding at Lustleigh could have been the perfect solution, as a camper carriage, which could accommodate up to six persons, was installed here in 1934 by the GWR.

The Great Western Railway, still revered by rail enthusiasts, was itself gobbled up under the umbrella of 'British Railways' in 1947. In the immediate postwar years this line continued to enjoy a healthy custom, but the advent of the 1950s, increased car ownership, and an ending of petrol rationing, saw a distinct tail-off in railway business.

The line closed on 2 March 1959, when the strains of 'Auld Lang Syne' were heard along the line, hundreds turning out to see the last train, which was packed to overflowing. The electric atmosphere was filled with the sounds of exploding detonators, of bugles and whistle calls, a cacophony of sound, a far from silent send-off. It was a sign of changed times, for the lack of column inches given to the reporting of the end of the line was in stark contrast to the way it had been greeted at its joyous beginning. This controversial closure was set against a backcloth of constructive defiance, because there were many who thought it would and could be saved. Canon O. M. Jones, of Teigngrace, was one of the champions in trying to save the line, but it was left to a 15-year-old, Richard Cottrell of Wellington, to summon a meeting to decide on the best course of action. The South Devon Railway Preservation Society was formed with the intention of restoring the line as a private enterprise, but the only use of the line, apart from a few special passenger trains, was for freight, up to Moreton until 1964 and to Bovey until 1971. The dreams and aspirations of local railway enthusiasts evaporated, and the lines between Heathfield and Bovey were taken up in 1971. Part of Bovey Tracey's bypass lies along the old trackbed of the railway. The station at Moreton is now the depot for Thompson & Sons, a road haulage company and therefore the antithesis of that slogan 'Let the train take the strain'.

There are many romantics in the world who fancy converting derelict stations into the most amazing of homes, and Lustleigh's station has been lovingly adapted into a private residence. Mike Jacobs bought it in 1972 and has added 'bits' to it. The old waiting room and booking office became a living room ('just the ticket') and the ladies' waiting room and toilet became a kitchen.

Parts of the line can be walked but much of it is on private land and would-be walkers are likely to be 'derailed' by irate owners intent on preserving their privacy if they try to intrude. However, the section north of Bovey, as far as Wilford Bridge, affords a pleasant walk but can be hard on the feet unless thick soles are worn. This is no substitute for the real thing, riding the railway in a train or even perhaps hurtling through the Wrey and Bovey valleys in a free-wheeling wagon 'neath the starry skies.

THE TEIGN VALLEY LINE – FROM HEATHFIELD TO EXETER

From Heathfield (Chudleigh Road) this line passed over the River Bovey, a tributary of the Teign, to reach the small halt at Chudleigh Knighton. Beyond, it kept company with the Teign, the curving line still straighter than the meandering river, to the next station at Chudleigh. Alas, the trackbed of the railway now lies below 'The Devon Expressway', the A38.

The Teign, which the railway crossed many times, forms the boundary, for the most part, of the northeastern side of the Dartmoor National Park. Just beyond Christow Station the railway veered away from the edge of Dartmoor to make its way eastwards to Exeter. Like many smaller branch lines, its running was often viewed as a casual but friendly operation, drivers being on first-name terms with many of the passengers.

In the 1930s, a pre-conservation-conscious era, hundreds of folk boarded trains at both Newton Abbot and Exeter to travel out to Christow to pick the daffodils found in great profusion in the flat meadows beside the Teign, an act of unwitting floral vandalism that brought their homes a splash of colour for just a short time. In the past, horse race meetings were staged close to Christow Station and many folk flocked here to enjoy Teign House Races, which were at their peak of popularity in the early 1890s.

This line serviced a large number of mines and quarries in the valley, and market days saw healthy numbers of people travelling to Exeter or Newton. The line generally followed a lowland route but many of the villages in the valley were high on the hillside, places like Trusham, Christow and Hennock 'up in the clouds'.

The line was first opened in 1882 but only as far north as Ashton, the through route to Exeter not coming into service until 1903, late in the development of the railway network. However, its eventual completion made it a useful facility because the main line from Exeter to Newton Abbot was often subject to the effects of stormy seas, subsiding red cliffs or floods. On such occasions trains could be diverted along the Teign Valley line. It meant that trains, like the Cornish Riviera Express, could continue their journeys and, unlike these days, buses were not needed to convey passengers between Newton Abbot and Exeter or around the problem.

The line closed to passenger traffic during the summer of 1958 and I count myself lucky to have been an eight-year-old passenger as the line saw out its last passenger days. The journey was a splendid one, one which really could be enjoyed. The myriad of misty memories are of leaving an urban, roof-top Exeter behind, greenery, deep cuttings, high embankments, pretty stations, and one extremely long dark tunnel. There are many other pictures of this railway in my books *The Teign Valley of Yesteryear, Parts I and II*, which pictorially depict this area as it was a while ago.

TOTNES TO ASHBURTON

The arrival of this railway, on 1 May 1872, was enthusiastically welcomed in the Dartmoor borderland and, if nothing else, it gave 1,500 of its poorest inhabitants a free tea! However, not everything was quite as harmonious as it could have been. Here are some extracts, including some extremely long sentences, taken from a local newspaper a few days after the opening festivities.

"The branch line from Totnes through Staverton and Buckfastleigh to Ashburton was opened for passenger traffic with much rejoicing on Wednesday and the inhabitants of these three towns are now in possession of that which they have laboured assiduously for more than twenty years past. For some reason, not very clearly explained, a little animosity sprung up between the inhabitants of Buckfastleigh and Ashburton, the consequence of which was that the residents of the first-named place formed a committee and set to work with a will to obtain subscriptions wherewith to furnish amusements in their midst on the opening day. They were successful in so far that during the afternoon and evening their pleasure field was much more thronged than that at Ashburton; their amusements were quite equal, and they had what the others had not – a bonfire and display of fireworks after dark. Nearly 1,500 of the poor of the neighbourhood had an ample tea provided for them gratuitously, and right heartily did they enjoy it. There was also during the day a procession with bands and flags through all the principal streets, and then all adjourned to a field provided for the occasion near the railway."

Ashburton's celebrations, likewise, were also recorded…

"However, the good folks of Ashburton had every cause to be satisfied with their little town… In North-street and its approaches fir trees were planted, triumphal arches erected, and flags and banners suspended across the street, whilst the houses on either side of the streets were decorated more or less by their occupants. At the Old Bull Ring festoons of flowers were suspended across the street and had a very beautiful effect. Of all the house decorations, however, that we noticed there was nothing to equal that of Mr E. Michelmore in West-street. It was very tasteful indeed. A band paraded the streets during the day, and the church bells rang out merry peals.

At about twelve o' clock the 'directors train' arrived at Buckfastleigh… They were driven to the King's Arms Hotel where one or two complimentary toasts were drunk in champagne, and the whole then returned to the station, arriving at Ashburton at about half-past one. Here they were met by a few of the townspeople and marched in procession to the Market Hall, headed by the Ashburton Rifle Band.

Generally speaking there are always some amusements to be derived from every novelty, and perhaps none more so than in the opening of a railway. That has, however, considerably decreased; still there are some rustics, and especially of the juvenile class, who have rarely, if ever, witnessed a locomotive with a string of carriages in its wake. On Wednesday we

noticed scores – old and young – who appeared to gaze on the puffing monster with awe, and who, if we may judge by countenances, seemed to wonder where the propelling power came from…

Of the line itself little need be said at our hands… If we are rightly informed the project had proceeded further than a mere talk of the matter – the route was staked out, but the needful [finance] could not be raised, hence it fell through. During the years 1864 and 1865 a further attempt was made and but for the exceeding assiduity of Mr John Hamlyn, a manufacturer of Buckfastleigh, there is no doubt that there would have been another failure. However by dint of great perseverance he succeeded in bringing his brother manufacturers and others in the neighbourhood to a sense of their duty and his efforts have been crowned with success, and there is now opened up to the tourist, picnic parties, lovers of shooting and fishing, and others one of the most delightful bits of country to be found in Devon. Although the contractors have here and there found obstacles in the shape of somewhat difficult cuttings, it has not been, on the whole, an arduous undertaking. It is an exceedingly pretty ride along the line, bordering as it does the serpentine Dart and Yeo [the River Ashburn] with their accompanying charming scenery and the neighbouring and outlying villages, dotted here and there in secluded valleys and on the sides of shaded hills. Some £75,000, we believe, has been expended in the construction of the line, but the excursion and goods traffic is expected to be large. There is a vast amount of serge material turned out in the neighbourhood, and besides this there are some extensive flour mills, limestone and slate quarries and numerous iron and other mines, the produce of which can be conveyed to their destination by rail much cheaper than by road…"

The Rev. T. Kitson had the right idea, during the loyal toasts, suggesting to the railway company that they

"… ought to treat the Bishop in a liberal way as a regular customer, since he was always travelling about wherever he could do any good; and as for rectors and curates, he hoped they would be conveyed over the railway cheap, as they didn't receive good salaries like railway directors." – (Laughter.)

Mr Tucker had other hopes and the paper reported:

"He anticipated that the opening of the line would bring large numbers of tourists to the neighbourhood to enjoy the magnificent drives which for fifteen miles along the Dart were, by the liberality of their chairman, Mr Bastard, thrown open to the public."

Mr Tucker directed his comments to the ancient, but 'sleepy' stannary town on the southern edge of Dartmoor.

"The railway, in his opinion, would be the means of awakening Ashburton from its period of slumbering, to one of increased prosperity. He believed this small line of railway, eight or nine miles in extent, would be equal … to some lines three times its length. Let them look at what would be carried over it. At Staverton thousands of hogsheads of cider were made and sent away. At Buckfastleigh there were the large works of Messrs. Berry and Son, and Messrs. Hamlyn, who did an immense trade. Then, in the vicinity of Buckfastleigh there were the Wheal Emma and the Brook Mines. The want of a railway was the cause of the resources at Ashburton not being fully developed … Other mines also in the neighbourhood were now to be worked in consequence of the railway being brought near … Umber had been discovered … and specimens of iron stone found had been submitted to a professor in London … then there were copper and tin mines … which no doubt would be worked… Then, if they considered the beautiful scenery that would be opened up, he thought that they would agree that the prospects of the line as regarded traffic were very encouraging."

Certainly the fine tea that followed, and the Grand Ball at the Golden Lion at Ashburton, did nothing to suggest that this branch line could one day, many years hence, conceivably close as an uneconomic venture. It's always as well that we can't see what the future holds!

Amy Jones MBE, born at Ashburton in 1889, was the first, but somewhat reluctant, lady Portreeve of Ashburton. She declined the offer of this prestigious post many times, until a keen gardener presented her with the most beautiful bowl of home-grown tomatoes that she had ever seen. Whilst she glowed over the gift, and nicely primed, he asked her once more. This time she couldn't refuse! Some years ago I had the pleasure of asking her about her memories of the railway and the town. She recalled that many of the townsfolk would visit the station even if they had no intention of catching the train, simply because it was such a picturesque place, the garden platforms so beautifully tended by the station staff that folk just wanted to savour the atmosphere there.

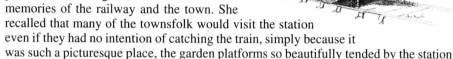

In the 1920s, when she was a schoolmistress at Bridgetown, Totnes, she would catch the train, fondly referred to as 'Bulliver' or 'Bolivar', to and from work. She knew the engine drivers so well that they would often allow her to ride on the footplate of the train and occasionally she drove the last few miles back to Ashburton! She also used to wave the flag or blow the whistle for the train's departure from Ashburton, the sorts of 'hands-on' experience that railway enthusiasts would have given a king's ransom to have had.

Here are some extracts from the *Western Morning News* report of 3 November 1958 of the branch line's noisy closure.

"To the accompaniment of fog signals, fireworks, whistles, and thunder and lightning the last passenger train on the Dart Valley branch line made noisy, but slow progress between Totnes and Ashburton on Saturday night. It carried about 700 passengers, including many local people who admitted they had never travelled on the line before, and also rail enthusiasts from as far away as London and Birmingham.

Earlier in the day, hundreds of enthusiasts had taken photos of the trains, all of which, starting with the midday trip from Totnes, consisted of five carriages and two locomotives instead of the usual one or two coaches.

Many people elected to say their goodbye during daylight so that they could obtain a last glimpse of the railway's view of the River Dart, but it was, of course, the last train which attracted the chief attention. The locomotives were 1466 and 1470, and one of them was driven by a member of the Ashburton Urban Council, Mr W. Cartwright. Ashburton was particularly well represented... None of the other places on the line was officially represented.

After an elaborate shunting movement at Totnes the last train left almost on time at 6.45 to the cheers of a small crowd. At once the fog signals and fireworks began to explode and nature contributed to the noise and flashes by producing a short thunderstorm.

Hundreds of people were gathered by the line to see the train pass ... The train being longer than the platform two stops were necessary at both the intermediate stations – Staverton and Buckfastleigh – where one of the mourners came dressed in a silk top hat... [and hopefully a bit more than that!]

Meanwhile, a crowd several hundred strong had formed at Ashburton and when the train came noisily to a standstill the platform was probably thronged with more people than ever before in its history – except on May Day, 1872, when the town welcomed its first train as the wonder of the age...

Officially the era was already over, but ... an unofficial return had to be run, and passengers were allowed to use it. About 250 did so. The departure from Ashburton again was accompanied by fireworks and cheering – and even by tears of people who loved the branch line so dearly that they found the tenor of the funeral distasteful..."

The former station building is still clearly recognisable but now it is the Station Garage.

The last leg from Buckfastleigh to Ashburton now lies somewhere under the tarmac of the Devon Expressway (A38) but the rest of the line still operates as the South Devon Railway, a private steam railway that delights thousands of visitors every summer. It has entertained many well-known passengers, John Alderton, the actor, being just one to travel the line purely for personal pleasure. The line has been used for many films and television programmes. *Lame Ducks*, which starred Lorraine Chase, Brian Murphy and John Duttine, was filmed at Staverton and in the surrounding countryside. In one of Michael Palin's *Ripping Yarns* Staverton, again, played the part of 'Torpoint', there being a touch of humour in this as most railway enthusiasts will know that Torpoint might have a ferry but it's never had a railway station! There are others who could be added to this list and they include Roy Hudd, Peter O'Toole and the Goodies.

David Soul, of *Starsky and Hutch* fame, came to the Dart Valley Railway (an earlier name) to shoot the classic silent-movie railway scene of a poor and distressed maiden tied to the railway lines with an onrushing train bearing down on her. Fortunately she is rescued by the hero just in time. However, in August 1991 an 'unofficial' video film was shot of the same story-line. Two ladies thought they could do some amateur filming after the last train of the day. What they didn't realise was that there was an unscheduled heavy engineering train working on the line. One of the ladies was the cameraman whilst the other, dressed only in frilly knickers and a revealingly sexy bra was shackled to the line. Luckily for them (and possibly for him!) a railway box office steward saw what was happening and after five frantic minutes released the lady tied to the line, just before the train came chugging around the blind bend where the filming was taking place. It was a close call!

FROM PLYMOUTH TO TAVISTOCK VIA THE PLYM VALLEY

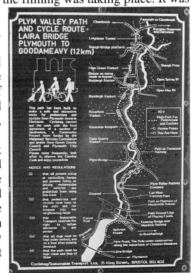

There used to be two ways of travelling by rail between Plymouth and Tavistock and both are considered briefly here. One still takes you part of the way and this one is a now a 'DIY' job; provided you have the pedal power, or the striding strength, you can pass along several miles of it.

The 16 miles of line from Plymouth to Tavistock (South), through the Plym Valley to Yelverton and then beyond, opened on a fine summer's day in late June 1859, the same year that Brunel finally bridged the Tamar at Saltash but also the one in which he died. The line was operated, initially, by the South Devon Railway Company, but was closely monitored by the seemingly all-powerful Great Western Railway.

What a terrific journey it must have been, the line branching off the main line at Marsh Mills ('Tavistock Junction') to follow the natural corridor of the heavily wooded Plym Valley towards the upland moors. Nevertheless there were four viaducts: Cann, originally a wooden trestle-work supported by stone piers, later rebuilt in Staffordshire brick; and three other granite structures, those of Riverford, Bickleigh and Ham Green with 5, 7 and 6 arches respectively. The long Shaugh Tunnel was also needed to enable the trains to climb up to the edge of Dartmoor proper. The line opened up the moors to the masses and on Bank Holidays, in the past, there was a mass exodus from this maritime city. At the peak of the line's popularity it was possible to get off at Marsh Mills, Plym Bridge (opened 1 May 1906), Bickleigh, Shaugh Bridge (19 August 1907), Clearbrook (29 October 1928), Yelverton, Horrabridge, Whitchurch Down or Tavistock or beyond to enjoy some moorland air.

Although this was generally a peaceful route there were occasional problems. In 1887 a train was derailed near Clearbrook, the engine driver was killed, and the fireman seriously injured.

Yelverton's station, before the First World War, saw plenty of activity, with a boost

in the numbers of people coming to the area for holidays or simply to improve their state of health. Hotels sprang up in this new settlement which, until the coming of the railway, had consisted of just a handful of buildings. The coming of the railway transformed it from being a remote place into one which was readily accessible and, as it turned out, a desirable location. Over the years the line saw some unusual 'passengers'. At one time Richard Woodman ran a thriving stable for racehorses, ones he exercised on Yennadon Down and Ringmoor Down. To get to meetings throughout the country, he found the most convenient form of transport to be the railway, and Yelverton was the chosen venue for 'the off'.

Having followed the Plym and Meavy valleys to Yelverton the railway then had to pass under the plateau of Roborough Down. An impressive 641-yard, virtually straight tunnel took the line on to the bustling Horrabridge station, high on the hill above its village, which had a busy goods yard and a large staff.

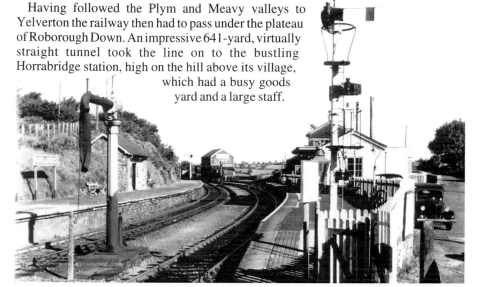

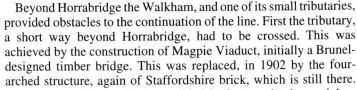

Beyond Horrabridge the Walkham, and one of its small tributaries, provided obstacles to the continuation of the line. First the tributary, a short way beyond Horrabridge, had to be crossed. This was achieved by the construction of Magpie Viaduct, initially a Brunel-designed timber bridge. This was replaced, in 1902 by the four-arched structure, again of Staffordshire brick, which is still there.

Magpie Viaduct enabled the line to maintain a straighter course, thus saving an extra sharp bend, to reach its 'jumping-off point' at the even larger Walkham Viaduct at Grenofen. Here a similar pattern followed. Brunel's original wooden viaduct, of exquisite beauty, spanned the Walkham, but was replaced, in 1910, by a more conventional viaduct, which also towered above the valley. Many bemoaned its passing when it was dismantled a few years after the closure of the railway. Beyond the Walkham the line passed through a pretty flower-filled cutting in the grounds of Grenofen House to enter the 374 yards long cavernous gloom of Grenofen Tunnel.

Probably the worst place of all a deaf person could choose to work would be on or right beside a railway line. Certainly for a Tavistock man, Nicholas Burnman, his lack of hearing was to be his undoing as he worked in a deep cutting on the Tavistock side of Grenofen Tunnel. The railway had been opened just five years when this well-weathered quarryman had been sent, by his boss, to work stone from this location. For the first few weeks of this task he worked in the company of another man but seemed able to adjust, even without the advantage of a watch or timepiece, to the daily, routine timetable of five trains and he continued his work alone. He seemed to instinctively know when to stand back, giving engine drivers a cheery wave as they passed him. But as is so often the case, in so dangerous a situation, one error of judgment can be fatal and this is how it resulted for poor Nicholas Burnman. The exact truth, of why he was hit by a train, can never be known, but the fact that it happened on a Friday may be a pointer. This has long been Tavistock's market day, a busy end to the week and one that drew so much business to the town that the railway company ran an extra mid-afternoon train. It is known, a witness having seen him working very close to the line a short time before, that he was struck by the 'recently established' 3.30 p.m. train from Tavistock which had left the market town about four minutes late. His badly mutilated body was later found inside Grenofen Tunnel, many yards along the line from where he had been working.

A few years after the closure of the line a strange incident occurred here, when three torch-carrying railway enthusiasts decided to explore the tunnel but one by one each strong beam inexplicably flickered out. It later transpired that the spot where this bizarre coincidence had occurred is where Mr Burnman's body was found. On hearing this another young man decided to explore the tunnel without a torch, feeling his way gradually into the darkness by following the wall. At the same spot he looked up in disbelief to spy a strange light ahead, on a side wall, this not being the other end of the tunnel! Simultaneously the ground beneath him began to shake violently and the loose ballast on the track started moving about like a small earthquake. Needless to say, the explorer beat a hasty retreat!

The line continued on to the small village of Whitchurch, which had its own halt, opened on 1 September 1906, before entering Tavistock.

'Tavistock South', which acquired this name on 26 September 1949, like its later counterpart of 'Tavistock North' on the LSWR line, was above the town centre. However, the original timber station of 1859 didn't last too long for a major fire, in Queen Victoria's Golden Jubilee Year of 1887, destroyed the building. It was an unfortunate porter who had inadvertently knocked over an oil lamp. The station was wisely rebuilt in stone.

The branch line continued on to Launceston via Lydford and we will consider some of this second part of its route later, as it followed a similar alignment to that of the former LSWR line for many moorland-edge miles.

The line between Tavistock South and Plymouth, which had opened with so much celebration, like a family greeting a new addition, appropriately went officially out of operation with a mock funeral at the end of December 1962. This railway, which had set out on a fine June day in 1859, closed in a blizzard on an austere, deep, dark December day, with several scheduled trains being cancelled, and with passengers marooned miles from home, three of them spending the night in the signal box at Bickleigh and others in the waiting room at Tavistock South... The 6.20 p.m. train from Plymouth to Tavistock arrived at 12.25 a.m. on Sunday morning, complete with a weather-beaten wreath attached to the front of the engine. What a cold 'Amen'!

PLYMOUTH TO TAVISTOCK VIA THE TAMAR AND TAVY VALLEYS

The 'other' way of getting to Tavistock from Plymouth was by another scenic route, part of which still survives as far as Bere Alston. The journey takes travellers above Devonport's dockyards and rooftops before skirting the Tamar bridges and river to travel beyond Tamerton Foliot, passing through some of the grandest scenery in our region. If you haven't done what's left of this journey then perhaps you should, before it's too late...

The LSWR were keen to expand their own network in the South West of England, and their completion of this line across the region opened up alternative possibilities to fruit producers in the Tamar Valley. The railway company's agents were quick to do deals to secure carrying contracts. It was not an uncommon sight to see trains with thirty carriages of fruit passing, London-bound, through Bere Ferrers.

But the line was also the scene of a large-scale tragedy. During the First World War ten New Zealand troops were killed on the line at Bere Ferrers, where they are remembered on a memorial in the lovely church of St Andrew's beside the Tavy estuary. A fuller account of this tragic story is included in another of my books, *Along the Tavy*.

The line, beyond the former mining village of Bere Alston, passed high along the side of the heavily wooded Tavy valley, through the dark and extremely damp Shillamill Tunnel, and crossed the Lumburn valley by the elegant and lofty Shillamill Viaduct to enter Tavistock. The town's station, 'Tavistock North', at the end of yet another towering viaduct, was a fine one for a small town.

Part of the trackbed of the railway, in this ancient Stannary Town, has been turned into a walk, and this passes over that high viaduct to give good views over the town centre. It is a 70-foot-high concrete structure faced in granite. One of the pillars, about twenty

feet above its base, has an arched aperture in it, a design feature to lessen the load on the foundations. However, those who lived in its shadow could never totally relax in the days when it was a working line… Sleepy Tavistock was almost given a jolt on 17 July 1961 when an incident occurred which could have been a major disaster. Indeed, one little old lady, who had retreated to the sanctuary of her outside loo, almost came a cropper, so to speak.

It was a Monday morning and the staff of the railway were getting through some routine railway maintenance work. The gangers were out on the line and were well aware of the various movements of the trains. They knew that old 'Cut-throat' would be past as he had been assigned the task of conveying condemned rolling stock from the station at Lydford on through Tavistock. His nickname had been bestowed on him by dint of his habit of leaning out of his cab and making the gesture of running his thumb across his neck. Apparently he was a most pleasant gentleman and this was just his little joke, a sort of personal 'trademark'.

As his long train reached Tavistock North station the wagons passed over a slight ridge on the railway which caused them to bounce and start coming off the line. Now had this been in the country, it would have been less of a problem, but here derailed trucks could have broken through the parapets of the large viaduct and crashed down onto the town houses below. The quick-thinking train driver accelerated and took the train and its wagons beyond the viaduct to safety. Had he braked sharply the consequences could have been disastrous. As it happens several of the wagons made contact with the sides of the bridge and bits of masonry were dislodged, most falling harmlessly to ground. However, our little old lady (whom you had probably forgotten by now!) was still ensconced in her outside loo in Taylor Square, unaware of the drama taking place high above on the lofty viaduct. Imagine the shock to her system as one stone penetrated the roof of the toilet and plummeted to the ground in front of her. Taken aback at the unexpected intrusion, she gazed skywards out of her 'loo with a view' to meet with the downward gaze of the railway gangers who had raced to the spot to see the extent of the damage. It appears (and this was a first-hand account) that several minutes later she was

still there, in all her glory, shaken but not stirred by the ordeal. Fortunately she recovered from this trauma. 'Cut-throat' was, apparently, given a commendation for his quick-witted handling of the incident.

During the First World War, as we have already seen, troop trains passed through Tavistock. On one occasion Canadian soldiers alighted from the train and, from the viaduct, tossed coins to the waiting youngsters down below, those not hit on the head grateful for their 'heaven-sent' gifts.

At one time the staff at the station wore smart uniforms with distinctive red ties. There were rumours that this colour has been specifically chosen so that in the event of an emergency they could be quickly removed and waved to signal a problem.

Both of Tavistock's railway stations had their peaks and troughs. On Goose Fair days there were scenes of sober sailors arriving *en masse*; but on leaving many were often

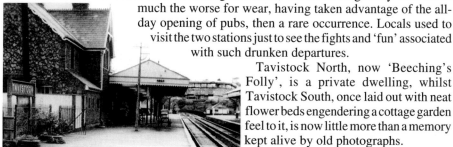

much the worse for wear, having taken advantage of the all-day opening of pubs, then a rare occurrence. Locals used to visit the two stations just to see the fights and 'fun' associated with such drunken departures.

Tavistock North, now 'Beeching's Folly', is a private dwelling, whilst Tavistock South, once laid out with neat flower beds engendering a cottage garden feel to it, is now little more than a memory kept alive by old photographs.

TAVISTOCK TO LYDFORD TIMES TWO!

It was also possible to get from Tavistock to Lydford by a choice of routes which ran very closely together between the two settlements. Rivalry between the two companies manifested itself in a number of ways.

At Mary Tavy and Blackdown's GWR station the station master wore a smart peaked cap complete with gold braid. By comparison his opposite number, on the Southern line at nearby Brentor, had a plain cap. Psychologically one wonders whether

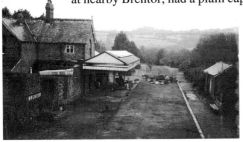

this would have made the GWR man feel more superior? Possibly not! An edition of the *Railway Magazine*, *circa* 1909, had this to say of the GWR station:

"Mary Tavy station is a contrast to Yelverton, for while the only non-original station has a lively aspect with wagonettes and victorias, and the Princetown branch traffic, Mary Tavy down platform is no longer used. In the summer of 1905 the writer saw the down platform used as a poultry run, all wired in. The then elderly station master, who has since died, was more than once reproved for the untidiness of this platform, and two or three special trains brought officials to see it. In the summer of 1906 the writer visited Mary Tavy, and found the platform prettily planted – not only the back of it, but just where piles of luggage were once meant to be. The signals are gone, and the signal box is used as a store, though there are two sidings and hand points. The London and South Western Railway runs through a cutting at the east side of this station, and has a station at Brentor instead… This part of the line is on the natural surface, and was cheap to construct, the land being open moor."

Today Brentor Station is a private home but retains its station appearance, and very smart it looks as well!

Nobody hears about railways when they run smoothly but when incidents occur they usually make front page headlines. In early March 1898 there was a major scare between Tavistock and Brentor when all of an Exeter to Plymouth train's carriages were derailed. Luckily everything remained upright and the train came to a standstill after several hundred yards.

There was another major incident in July 1927 about a mile from Brentor, on one of the line's steeper sections. A goods train was derailed and the 25 wagons were 'smashed to smithereens'; their contents – wood, coal, hay and other items – were strewn all over the place.

In the past the people of Mary Tavy and Brentor could often tell what the weather was like in the district by listening to approaching locomotives. If those coming from the Tavistock direction could be heard more clearly than ones coming from Lydford then rain was on the way. However, if the reverse was the case then colder, drier weather was more likely. It was not uncommon for two trains travelling in the same direction to race each other, timetables taking a back seat in such circumstances.

Lydford, like Tavistock, had two lines and two stations, one higher than the other. This also appeared in an edition of a railway magazine from 1909.

"Lydford station is, as far as the Great Western Railway is concerned, the second and by far the higher summit on the branch. Brentor hill is a prominent object in the view at Lydford station looking south. There are up and down platforms for each railway, and a junction from the London and South Western to the Great Western Railway, which forms the original means by which the London and South Western Railway reached Plymouth. The GWR is single from Marsh Mills, though the majority of the bridges over the line are sufficient width for a double line. The London and South Western Railway is, of course, double all the way between Lydford and Friary, Plymouth, though even now the L&SWR has to run over the GWR line in Plymouth for two miles. It is the penalty of getting there too late in the day. Lydford village, church and castle, are 1½ miles north of the station, and had the first railway in this district been built to connect Tavistock with Okehampton, no doubt the station would have been much nearer the village, and the tremendous curve between Tavistock and Launceston would have seemed more reasonable, but the configuration of the country made it necessary to go nearly 19 miles instead of barely 14 by road. The L&SWR had got to Okehampton by 29 August 1871. Mr Herbert Rake says that the L&SWR was completed as far as Lydford in 1873; but Mr Gibbons, who put all he could at my disposal ... gives 2 November 1874, as the date of opening ... to Lydford. The L&SWR trains began running to Plymouth over the GWR line on 17 May 1876 ceasing to do so on their line by way of Bere Alston in 1889.

Lydford is a delightful moorland resort, and ought to be much more visited … The L&SWR down trains can be heard roaring along as they rush down the gradient from Bridestowe, while the GWR trains from Coryton pass outside the garden of the hotel… From Lydford to Coryton the line is on the left side of the Lyd stream, and the line is through woods, gradually dropping down to the lower lands near the Tamar."

Observant road users travelling the A386 from Tavistock to Okehampton may have noticed on the eastern side of this route, near Bearslake, an impressive viaduct below the high moors of Lake Down. This is Lake Viaduct, where a public right of way passes under it. I do many talks around the county, usually about specific books I have written. At the end of a talk about the South Devon coastline, at a Women's Institute meeting, one respectable 'senior' lady shared a few of her railway memories with me. Apparently her first child, born in the 1930s, was conceived under this viaduct when she was on her honeymoon; had it been a boy she would have given him the middle name 'Lake'. In fact she had a daughter whom she named 'Virginia'.

Farther along the line towards Okehampton the railway had to be carried across the steep-sided West Okement valley. Lofty Meldon Viaduct was the answer to bridging this 160-foot-high gap, but it wasn't welcomed by everybody. Some local ladies christened it the 'Spider Bridge' on account of its appearance and vowed that they would never cross it 'as long as they lived'. In its last years of carrying passenger traffic there was a strict speed limit of 10 m.p.h. over this high-flying viaduct, just one of a few all-metal bridges in Britain.

Okehampton Station (750 feet asl) was, like Tavistock North, a busy one. Hundreds of thousands of holidaymakers would have passed through here in its working years. The likes of Sir John Betjeman (1906–1984), who adored railways, often caught the Atlantic Coast Express to the Cornish coast. He so loved Padstow and the Camel estuary that he was buried at St Enodoc, near the estuary's mouth. It's now possible to walk or cycle from Wadebridge along the former railway's trackbed to Padstow on part of 'the Camel Trail' and this is, without doubt, one of the best walks or bike rides in South West England. There were many places on the 'Southern' line that holidaymakers, complete with big brown seasoned suitcases secured with string and sentiment, with their excited children, the bucket and spade brigade, in tow, could travel to beyond Okehampton.

In 1947 the town was honoured by the railway company when a West Country class locomotive, No 21c113, was named 'Okehampton'. It was a wonderful locomotive which was built at Brighton and weighed 128 tons. At that time the Atlantic Coast Express left Waterloo to make the 260-mile journey to Padstow in a fast time, reaching speeds of some 80 miles per hour, this being regarded as pretty quick in those days. It would leave London at 11.00 a.m. every weekday and its regular nine to eleven coaches could accommodate 396 passengers. At Okehampton portions of trains could be divided or combined. The goods shed had 14 bays and the station, at its peak, was a busy one. The last ACE to pass through was in September 1964.

The railway, still used by mineral trains from Meldon Quarry, and the occasional

passenger train between Okehampton and Exeter, soon passes over another impressive structure, Fatherford Viaduct, straddling the East Okement river. In the past this stood as a distinct landmark; but with the building of the Okehampton By-pass it has lost its individuality because now it is 'accompanied' across the valley by a road bridge. Below these towering bridges is a beauty spot frequented mostly by locals who enjoy walks in the steep, wooded East Okement valley.

The railway had reached out gradually to Okehampton; the Coleford Junction to North Tawton section, an extremely straight one, opened in 1865 whilst the line on to Okehampton was not established until 3 October 1871. The station for Sampford Courtenay, again in the shadow of Dartmoor's highest peaks, was known initially as Okehampton Road, but became Belstone Corner in October 1871 only to change, yet again, a few months later, on 1 January 1872, to Sampford Courtenay. It was here, in 1906, that the two perpetrators of Okehampton's biggest ever burglary, Harry Groves and James Long (the first ever committed by thieves using a battery torch) boarded the train bound for Exeter and what they imagined to be a clean getaway. However, the fact that they are named here means that all didn't go exactly to plan… If you would like to know more then you should read *Okehampton Collection II,* the second of Mike and Hilary Wreford's trilogy of old pictures and anecdotes about Okehampton.

THE YELVERTON–PRINCETOWN LINE

A comment applied to a lot of disused railways is that, had they been kept open, they would have become major tourist attractions today, which – to a degree – is probably true. The one line which would have offered the best ride and views of upland Dartmoor, had it not closed in March 1956, was the branch from Yelverton to Princetown. It was a line that had been 'tagged on' to the line from Plymouth to Tavistock (South) in 1883, the same year that the Dartmoor Preservation Association was formed, and was expected to serve a number of functions.

Princetown, windblown, rain-lashed and somewhat austere, is the highest 'town' in Devon, a place that is often shrouded in mist, its grim prison a salutary reminder that it's better to be on the right side of the law. For some 73 years it was literally the end of the line for some offenders.

The passenger line was not initiated with all the pomp and ceremony lavished on other railways. Indeed, as this report from the *Western Morning News* on 19 August 1883 shows us, the highest railway in Devon commenced with the lowest of profiles, unlike its last working day when it seemed like 'the world and his wife' wanted to ride on it.

"The passenger trains between Horrabridge and Princetown did begin running on Saturday, and the railway has at last penetrated into the heart of Dartmoor. With such little definite warning did this event occur that the inhabitants had no time to prepare for the celebration of the event. In fact, up till a late hour the previous day no one seems to have known anything about it, and then the news did not go much beyond the Plymouth offices of the Great Western Railway Company. Singularly enough the fact does not appear to have been communicated to the contractor, Mr Mackey, and the first train as announced in the time tables, and advertised in the newspapers could not be run because the contractor, not knowing anything about it, had two or three engines upon the line, with men doing work not yet complete. It is not known why the line was opened with this precipitancy. It appears, however, that the company took it for granted that Colonel Yolland would be satisfied with all the arrangements, and that there not be the slightest doubt about the company being able to open the line on Saturday... But there arose a hitch concerning the sufficiency of Horrabridge Station as a junction, and the Board of Trade seems to have thought so seriously of it that it was not until the last moment that the railway authorities were sure they would be able to carry out their arrangements, and commence running their trains on Saturday. They were only allowed to do so, it is stated, conditionally. Within a specified time they must either make a station at Yelverton or double the station accommodation at Horrabridge.

From the circumstances already explained the 11.20 train from Plymouth and 12.8 from Horrabridge was the first train that ever carried passengers to Princetown. The writer used the first ticket issued from North Road to Princetown, and paid for it the sum of 1s 11¹/₂d [just under ten pence]... The junction of the new line is at Yelverton, which has long been a signal station, where trains crossed each other, and is about two miles on the Plymouth side of Horrabridge. Whatever the cause may be, it remains a fact that there is no station at present at Yelverton. For their own convenience, therefore, the railway company will take you on to Horrabridge and bring you back again to Yelverton, and charge additional mileage fare for it. Another singular and misleading statement will be found upon the tickets themselves. They are issued from Plymouth to Princetown 'via Bickleigh.' Evidently the designer of these tickets was under the impression that to take passengers to Princetown via Horrabridge was an arrangement inconsistent with common sense and rectified it in print before the company are prepared to rectify it in fact. We believe, however, they are anxious to do this as soon as possible.

The scenery of the new line ... is exceedingly picturesque and grand. Having started from Horrabridge and obtained the necessary staff at Yelverton, the train gets upon the new line. From this point to Princetown its extreme length is ten miles and a half, and it almost continues to rise the whole of the way. Leaving the junction the train rounds a sharp curve on an embankment twenty feet high, and extending for three eighths of a mile. A cutting is then entered about thirty five feet deep, the deepest cutting on the line; when the train emerges ... the valley in which Meavy Church and village are situated opens out to the right. The line here crosses the Devonport leat, and gets on the bank of the old Princetown tramway, and still rises up to the first station on the line, which is called 'Dousland' – not Dousland

Barn, the name by which the locality is known. This is just about a mile and a half from the junction. The Dousland Station buildings are very neat. Starting from Dousland, the line again rapidly rises. Mr A. P. Prowse's house is passed on the left, and there is a level crossing nearby. The line wends around Yennadon Down, and twists along in a serpentine course until the Sheepstor valley comes in view. The Plymouth leat here runs just below the line and the Devonport leat just above it. Crossing over the Sheepstor and Lawrey roads, the line next emerges on Peek Hill, going over the main road to Princetown by a solid granite arch... Then the line again begins to climb, and rises continuously until Princetown is reached. The steepest gradient is 1:41. When the line gets on Walkhampton Common a beautiful expanse of country lies, open to the westwards, a glimpse being obtained of the Tamar, and of Cornish hills beyond, while Walkhampton Church and the village of Horrabridge lie nestling immediately below. At a high point on Walkhampton Common, a siding, with signals and other accommodation has been made for the convenience of that immediate district, and being on a high level, it is thought it will be of considerable advantage to the farmers and others for heavier goods, as it will obviate a great deal of hill. Then, going along

the moor practically on the lines of the old tramway, the line first of all rounds Ingletor [sic] and then King Tor near the summit. A little further on, and still rising, the line reaches Foggin Tor Granite Quarries, similar works upon King Tor having previously been passed. Here Mr Pethick has been anticipating events by getting some-

thing like eight hundred tons of granite pitching ready for being despatched to Plymouth. A little further up are the Swell Tor Granite Quarries; and here looking to the westward, the peculiar nature of the line is well illustrated. Barely a quarter of a mile below is the line which has previously been travelled, the train in the meantime having gone about three miles round the hill, and the line having in that distance risen 150 feet. Another five minutes brings us into Princetown, the line then having risen to the height of 850 feet above Yelverton, and 1,350 feet above sea level. Between the station at Dousland and the Princetown Station the distance is about eight miles. By the extensive way in which the station premises are laid out it is evident that a considerable amount of traffic is anticipated at Princetown. There is a capital goods shed, four times as large as the one at Dousland, an engine-house for two

engines, a turn-table, and a carriage shed 180 feet long. Wide approach roads for both passengers and goods are made into the middle of Prince-town, the road across the Green to the Duchy Hotel having been widened and utilised. The station provision at Dousland is said to .... afford no accommodation for excursion trains.

Although the notice was so short, the trains that ran on Saturday were well patronised. The passengers by the 12.8 train from Horrabridge ... was driven by Mr John Goodall, the foreman engineer of the district. Owing to the peculiar character of the line, the trains require careful driving, and every confidence is placed in Mr Williams, the driver selected for the line. Mr Higman, from Launceston, has been appointed station master at Princetown, and the traffic will ordinarily be superintended by Inspector Chamberlain, of Tavistock. A large number of people assembled to witness the arrival and departure of each train at Princetown, but as already stated the notice was too short to allow of any demonstration being organised on Saturday. It is announced by advertisement that festivities both at Dousland and Princetown are fixed for Wednesday. At the latter place a tea will be given to the children; there will also be a public tea and a number of sports, and the proceedings will be wound up by a display of fireworks.".

Dousland may have been a neat, even picturesque station but not everybody was taken with it. One Edwardian travel writer wrote: "

Dousland signal-box is of stone with rather gloomy-looking cement, as is the station, the cement being Roman cement, which looks anything but pleasing, of greenish greyish brown – greenish owing to vegetable matter in Roman cement and as the outside woodwork is painted brown and made to look like grained wood, the colour scheme does not please everybody. The cement reminds one of very wet winters, and this station is much exposed to the south-west wind."

The addition of a number of halts later opened up Dartmoor to those who wanted to walk the hills and tors. 'Burrator and Sheepstor', with an exceedingly long name board but relatively short platform, opened in 1924, was regarded as one of the most beautiful locations in the entire country for such a stop. The picture here, taken in 1926, shows the temporary viaduct which was strung across Burrator Lake during the raising of the dam wall to increase the reservoir's capacity.

In 1928 King Tor Halt, useful for a few years to those who lived in the group of quarry-men's houses nearby, was established, and finally the halt at Ingra Tor was added in 1936 in a decade that saw many of the granite quarries of Dartmoor cease operating. This halt had a sign, now famous in railway folklore for its total lack of punctuation. The precise wording stated: "IN THE INTERESTS OF GAME PRESERVATION AND FOR THEIR PROTECTION AGAINST SNAKES ETC DOGS SHOULD BE KEPT ON A LEAD BY ORDER." It is now housed at Saltram House.

The line ran for ten miles and 46 chains between Yelverton and Princetown, two places just six miles apart. The great difference in altitude meant that the engineers, using much of the route of a previous horse-drawn railway, were obliged to contour the hillsides, not daring to attempt a gradient any steeper than 1:40. This constraint meant that immense meanders around the hillsides were necessary. Still, it guaranteed that views in almost every direction were presented to those who were fortunate to have travelled this line. Sometimes, though, these bends posed a challenge to walkers. At the beginning of one of these giant loops, at Yes Tor Bottom, it was possible to get off the train and walk up the hillside to meet the train again at King Tor Halt within about 13 minutes. Those who stopped to tie up their boots, admire the moor or dither too long missed the train. The average journey time from Yelverton to Princetown was about 41 minutes, the reverse journey being some 6 minutes less on average, this being a reflection of the slowness of the train in climbing steadily for so long.

The Great Blizzard of 1891 is one often quoted in the history books. Although not the coldest spell of weather on record, an incredible amount of snow fell in March. An evening train, with a single coach and just a small number of passengers, became stranded for two long nights. The engine driver admitted that "We ought never to have started". The carriages were full of snow up to the hat racks and the train was almost buried. Fortunately a farmer rescued the passengers and crew and escorted them to a nearby farm.

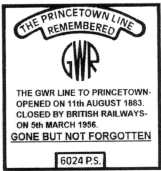

Even as late as the Second World War the uplands of Dartmoor still remained relatively remote, and residents of Yeo Farm, below the line in the Meavy valley, usually only got to hear world news quite a time after it happened. However, as the war drew to a close they became desperately keen to know when the hostilities ceased, so arranged with the engine driver on the Princetown line that as soon as peace was declared he would sound his whistle when rounding Yennadon Down, high above the farm. When this eventually occurred there was much rejoicing in the Yeo Farm household.

The upper part of the line is fully accessible to walkers but is also used by mountain bikers, some faster than the trains which once ran here! Dartmoor letterboxers, that breed of walker who spend much of their moorland safaris looking for hidden 'letterboxes' having been given cryptic clues and various directions, have also followed this line. A series of special letterbox stamps to coincide with the fortieth anniversary of the last scheduled passenger train to trundle along this 'alpine' railway were put out in March 1996 by the '6024 Preservation Society'. There were 11, each headed 'The Princetown Line Remembered', which included illustrations of the stations and halts, the last rail crew and other items to do with the line's running.

THE GWR LINE TO PRINCETOWN- OPENED ON 11th AUGUST 1883. CLOSED BY BRITISH RAILWAYS- ON 5th MARCH 1956.

GONE BUT NOT FORGOTTEN

6024 P.S.

That last railway journey, in early March 1956, was again well patronised and extra carriages had to be put on to accommodate the crowds. It was a cold, murky day which did not show off the railway at its best. At Princetown many passengers were subjected to a wait on a chilly platform whilst the crew shunted the last delivery of milk into the goods shed. However, die-hard rail enthusiasts hardly noticed the elements, their attention fully given to the railway that they loved. Nevertheless this last day saw thousands descend on the line, and at Yelverton there was chaos caused by the great influx of sightseers.

Many people have mourned the passing of this and many of the other railway lines which have now vanished into history. The majority of those 'Railways on and around Dartmoor' are deserted, and those which are still accessible now only see walkers, horse riders and mountain bikers. Much former railway land has reverted back to private ownership and access to many stretches of railroad is now either difficult or impossible. In places, some sections have become overgrown jungles of impenetrable vegetation, whilst in others even the occasional pig farm has been established where once trains trundled along. On that inauspicious porcine note we, too, have run out of steam and come to the end of the line!